THE MAGIC OF LANGUAGE

Adverbs

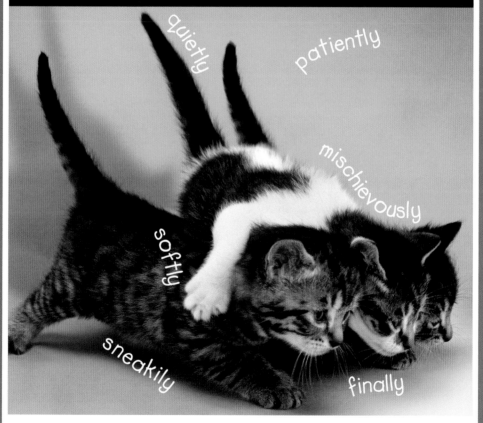

By Ann Heinrichs

THE CHILD'S WORLD®
CHANHASSEN, MINNESOTA

Published in the United States of America by The Child's World®
PO Box 326, Chanhassen, MN 55317-0326
800-599-READ
www.childsworld.com

Content Adviser:
Kathy Rzany, M.A.,
Adjunct Professor,
School of Education,
Dominican University,
River Forest, Illinois

Photo Credits: Cover photograph: Punchstock/Digital Vision Interior photographs:
Animals Animals/Earth Scenes: 7 (Donald Specker), 15 (McDonald Wildlife
Photography); Corbis: 5 (Paul A. Sounders), 9, 10 (Reuters NewMedia Inc.), 14
(Dale C. Spartas), 16 (Will & Deni McIntyre); Getty Images/Digital Vision: 13;
Getty Images/Stone: 20 (Ron Krisel), 27 (Siegfried Layda); PictureQuest: 21
(Richard Orton/Index Stock Imagery), 23 (Dan Snipes/Stock Connection);
Punchstock/Digital Vision: 25.

The Child's World®: Mary Berendes, Publishing Director

Editorial Directions, Inc.: E. Russell Primm, Editorial Director; Pam Rosenberg,
Project Editor; Melissa McDaniel, Line Editor; Katie Marsico, Assistant Editor; Matt
Messbarger, Editorial Assistant; Susan Hindman, Copyeditor; Susan Ashley and Sarah
E. De Capua, Proofreaders; Chris Simms and Olivia Nellums, Fact Checkers; Timothy
Griffin/IndexServ, Indexer; Cian Loughlin O'Day and Dawn Friedman, Photo
Researchers; Linda S. Koutris, Photo Selector

The Design Lab: Kathleen Petelinsek, Design and Page Production;
Kari Thornborough, Page Production Assistant

Library of Congress Cataloging-in-Publication Data
Heinrichs, Ann.
  Adverbs / by Ann Heinrichs.
     p. cm. — (The magic of language)
Includes index.
Contents: What is an adverb?—How to hop, when to leave, where to go—How cool
was that concert?—Adverbs helping adverbs—Which dog barks more loudly?—
Barking the most loudly of all—Where does the adverb go?—Acting like an adverb—
It's real, really!—Singing badly, smelling good.
  ISBN 1-59296-069-3 (library bound : alk. paper)
  1. English language—Adverb—Juvenile literature. [1. English language—Adverb.]
I. Title. II. Series: The Magic of Language.
  PE1325.H38 2004
  428.2—dc22   2003020039

TABLE OF CONTENTS

CHAPTER ONE

WHAT IS AN ADVERB?

DEFINITION

An **adverb** is a word that modifies a verb, an adjective, or another adverb.

Suppose a kangaroo got loose in your neighborhood. You'd have lots of questions. How did it happen? When did it escape? Where did it go? You might learn the answers from adverbs.

EXAMPLE

Today, a kangaroo **boldly** ripped its cage **wide open** and sprang out.

My **bright** green turtle **simply** crawled **away yesterday**.

Auntie Annie lives **here rather quietly now**.

All the blue words above are adverbs. They modify verbs,

How and when did this kangaroo escape? Where did he go? Adverbs have the answers! He escaped easily, he did it today, and he ended up here!

adjectives, or other adverbs. What does *modify* mean? It means to

describe another word or change its meaning in some way. An adverb

might puff up a word **(extremely)** or tone it down **(hardly).**

Adverbs often answer the questions "how?" or "when?" or "where?"

Which adverbs in the examples on page 4 answer these questions?

HOT
TIP

Most "how" adverbs end in -ly—slowly, quietly, loudly, tightly, cheerfully, truly, patiently, boldly, suddenly. They're formed by adding -ly to adjectives—slow, quiet, loud, and so on. What if an adjective ends with -y? In most cases, you form the adverb by taking away the -y and adding -ily—easy/easily, angry/angrily, happy/happily, and so on.

Want More?

The "when" adverbs include: **now,**

yesterday, today, tomorrow,

soon, recently. There are lots of

"where" adverbs—**here, there,**

everywhere, anywhere

nowhere, far, nearby,

away, outside, inside, out, in, up, down.

Do pigeons like these ever roost on your windowsill? How often? Your answer could be one of these adverbs—always, sometimes, never, usually, often.

Some adverbs answer the question "how often?"

EXAMPLE

Uncle Ted **always** brings us candy corn.

Pigeons **sometimes** roost on my windowsill.

You **never** take the garbage out.

Other adverbs answer "to what extent or degree?"

EXAMPLE

Joshua is **slightly** taller than Jonah.

I'd be **extremely** happy to make a B on the test.

That kangaroo was **terribly** hungry!

CHAPTER TWO

HOW TO HOP, WHEN TO LEAVE, WHERE TO GO

Some adverbs modify verbs.

These adverbs tell something

about the action.

QUICK FACT

A verb is an action word.

EXAMPLE

The kangaroo hopped **wildly** across the lawn.

It left the zoo **recently.**

It managed to go **everywhere!**

Hopped, left, and **go** are verbs, or action words. What do

the adverbs tell about those actions? Just ask how, when, and where

the actions took place.

EXAMPLE

QUESTIONS ABOUT THE VERBS	ANSWERS (ADVERBS)
How did it **hop?**	wildly
When did it **leave?**	recently
Where did it **go?**	everywhere

CHAPTER THREE

HOW COOL WAS
THAT CONCERT?

If you want to make a strong point, use an adverb! Adverbs work

wonders when they modify adjectives.

Adverbs add extra meaning to an adjective.

They can make the adjective sound way more

important—or less important.

QUICK FACT

An adjective is a word that modifies, or describes, a noun or pronoun.

*This girl is telling a story. It's not just a long story. It's a really long story.
The adverb really adds extra meaning to the adjective long.*

Britney's hair is completely blond, and her concert was totally cool. The adverbs completely and totally help make a strong point.

EXAMPLE

Britney's hair is **completely** blond.
The concert was **totally** cool.
My hands are clean **enough!**

In these examples,

blond, cool, and

clean are adjectives. See

how the adverbs affect the

adjectives? These questions

show how the adverbs add

extra meaning.

EXAMPLE

QUESTIONS ABOUT THE ADJECTIVES	ANSWERS (ADVERBS)
How **blond** is Britney's hair?	**completely** blond
How **cool** was that concert?	**totally** cool
How **clean** are your hands?	clean **enough**

CHAPTER FOUR

ADVERBS HELPING ADVERBS

Some adverbs modify other adverbs. Here are some examples:

EXAMPLE

The snake slinks **so** smoothly through the grass.
Cheetahs run **incredibly** fast.
The tooth fairy visits me **fairly** often.
The singer arrived **too** late for his show.

In these examples, **smoothly, fast, often,** and **late** are adverbs. They all modify verbs. Notice how each of these adverbs is modified by another adverb.

EXAMPLE

QUESTIONS ABOUT THE ADVERBS	ANSWERS (MORE ADVERBS)
How **smoothly?**	**so** smoothly
How **fast?**	**incredibly** fast
How **often?**	**fairly** often
How **late?**	**too** late

CHAPTER FIVE

WHICH DOG BARKS MORE LOUDLY?

DEFINITION

The **comparative form** of an adverb compares two things.

Skipper barks loudly, but Hoover barks more loudly.

This example shows how you can use adverbs to compare two things.

If two kids run **fast,** one probably runs **faster.** If two turtles crawl **slowly,** one probably crawls **more slowly.**

If you and your friend eat **quickly,** one of you probably eats **more quickly!** All these adverbs are modifying verbs.

Don't forget—adverbs can modify adjectives, too. In this

There are lots of ways to describe these kids using comparative adverbs. Both are running fast, but one is running faster. Both are shouting loudly, but one is shouting more loudly. Can you think of more ways to describe them using comparative adverbs?

example, **brown** is an adjective. It's modified by the comparative

adverb **darker.**

Here comes a darker brown horse.

Like comparative

adjectives, some adverbs

build the comparative

form by adding *-er,* as in

faster and **harder.**

However, most compara-

tive adverbs use **more**

or **less,** as in **more**

beautifully and

less patiently.

This horse's sister is dark brown, but he is even darker brown. The comparative adverb darker modifies the adjective brown.

*This bear is eating **as quickly as** it can! Maybe it found the food **earlier than** its playmates did. The comparative adverbs in these sentences help you describe how and when the monkey does things.*

Comparative adverbs share some other things with comparative adjectives. They use **than** when comparing two different things.

If the two things are similar, **as . . . as** is used.

Mr. Wu arrived **earlier than** his daughter.
The baby bear ate **more greedily than** its mother.
Do you study math **as seriously as** grammar?
We got here **as quickly as** we could.

CHAPTER SIX

BARKING THE MOST LOUDLY OF ALL

DEFINITION

The **superlative form** of an adverb compares three or more things.

You can use superlative adverbs to compare three or more people, such as the students in this classroom. In your opinion, which student tries the hardest? Which one thinks the most deeply? Which one studies the longest? It's hard to tell, isn't it?

Skipper barks loudly, and Hoover barks more loudly, but Mollie barks the most loudly of all.

What if three or more dogs are barking loudly? You compare them by using the superlative form of the adverb.

Of all your classmates, one works **the hardest.** Think about your shoes. Which pair fits **the most comfortably?** Do you like early-morning cartoons? Which one begins **the earliest** of all?

As you see, **the** usually comes before a superlative adverb. Like superlative adjectives, some superlative adverbs are formed by adding *-est.* Other superlatives use **most** or **least.**

Alissa runs the farthest of anyone and tries the hardest.
Roberto cheers the most often and the least timidly.

A few adverbs have irregular comparative and superlative

forms. They don't add *-er* or *-est,* and they don't use more, less,

most, or least. Some examples are **well–better–best** and

badly–worse–worst.

TRY THESE!

Name the comparative and superlative forms of these adverbs:

clearly   soon   happily   late   cheaply

See page 32 for the answers. Don't peek!

WATCH OUT!

Never use a double comparison. One is enough! You would never say more easier or most fastest.

WATCH OUT!

Some adverbs cannot be compared. They're already as extreme as they can get. You would never say, "This usually always happens." If it always happens, there's no "usually" about it!

CHAPTER SEVEN

WHERE DOES THE ADVERB GO?

Some parts of speech have to be in one certain place. But adverbs are often free to jump around. Just look at these examples. No matter where the adverb is, the meaning stays the same.

Slowly the tiger turned toward me.
The tiger **slowly** turned toward me.
The tiger turned **slowly** toward me.
The tiger turned toward me **slowly.**

What if there's more than one possible word the adverb might modify? Then put the adverb closest to the word it modifies. Notice how the position of the adverb changes the meaning.

Bozo **quietly** strolled in, turned a somersault, and left.
Bozo strolled in, **quietly** turned a somersault, and left.
Bozo strolled in, turned a somersault, and **quietly** left.

"I grew only one inch!"

WATCH OUT!

Don't say, "I only grew one inch." This way, the adverb **only** modifies the verb **grew**. It means you grew, and you didn't do anything else. You didn't eat or sleep or play. You only grew! Instead, say "I grew **only one inch**." Here, **only** modifies the adjective **one**.

Sometimes an adverb modifies a whole sentence. Then it's usually placed at the beginning of the sentence. A comma separates it from the rest of the sentence.

EXAMPLE

Unfortunately, the candy store is closed.
Frankly, I don't care.
Luckily, I have plenty of candy at home!

CHAPTER EIGHT

ACTING LIKE AN ADVERB

A noun is a naming word. But sometimes a noun acts like an adverb. Noun words behave like adverbs when they tell how, when, or where.

How many nouns can you name in this picture? Kids, playground, and ladder are all nouns because they are names of persons, places, or things.

NOUN	ADVERB
Welcome to my **home!**	He went **home.**
Tuesday is my birthday.	We play every **Tuesday.**

Some words can be either adjectives or adverbs. How can you tell which it is? Try the simple adverb test. Ask if the word tells how, when, or where. If it does, it's an adverb. If it modifies a noun or pronoun, it's an adjective.

ADJECTIVE	The **early** bird catches the worm.
ADVERB	The bird got up **early.**

ADJECTIVE	We ate in a **nearby** diner.
ADVERB	We found its nest **nearby.**

ADJECTIVE	Where's the **next** batter?
ADVERB	I'm batting **next.**

ADJECTIVE	He's in **first** grade.
ADVERB	Cameron got here **first.**

ADJECTIVE	She threw a **hard** ball.
ADVERB	I hit that ball really **hard.**

These boys are playing outside. In this case, outside is an adverb. What if they are playing outside their own backyard? Then outside is a preposition.

Some words can be either prepositions or adverbs. It's pretty easy to tell which is which. All prepositions are followed by an object. Together, the preposition and its object form a tight little bundle of information.

EXAMPLE

PREPOSITION	Think **outside** the box.
ADVERB	I'm playing **outside**.
PREPOSITION	Paul sat **in** the car.
ADVERB	Three lizards scurried **in**.
PREPOSITION	Maria went **out** the door.
ADVERB	The monkey hopped **out**.

CHAPTER NINE

IT'S REAL—REALLY!

Are you **real** happy today? No! You're **really** happy! Does your best friend treat you **nice?** No way! Your friend treats you **nicely!** But your happiness is **real,** and your friend is **nice.**

It's easy to mix up adjectives and adverbs. Let's un-mix them right now! **Real** and **nice** are adjectives. They modify nouns or pronouns. **Really** and **nicely** are adverbs. They modify verbs, adjectives, or other adverbs.

These examples show the proper use of adjectives:

EXAMPLE

This ring is made of **real** gold.
Docker is a **slow** horse.
Jessica let out a **loud** meow.
Ms. Hernandez is **nice.**
We spotted a **bright** star named Polaris.

All the blue words page 24 are adjectives. But watch out! Those same words cannot modify verbs, adjectives, or adverbs. They don't tell how, when, or where. Only adverbs can do that! To change those adjectives into

Why does this cat meow so loudly? It's hard to tell, but we do know that the adverb loudly modifies the verb meow.

adverbs, add -*ly*. Here's how to use the adverb forms properly:

EXAMPLE

RIGHT	WRONG
We were **really** tired last night.	real tired
Carmen tried **really** hard to score.	real hard
Jumpy moves **slowly.**	moves slow
Fluffy meows **loudly.**	meows loud
Play **nicely,** children.	play nice
The stars are shining **brightly.**	shining bright

Be sure to use the right comparative and superlative forms, too.

Remember—only an adverb can modify a verb!

RIGHT		WRONG
(ADVERB)		(ADJECTIVE)
Try to move **more quickly!**		quicker
A full moon shines **the most brightly.**		the **brightest**
My cat meows **more loudly** than yours.		louder

TRY THESE!

Choose the correct adjective or adverb in these sentences. The adjective is the first choice, and the adverb is second. Does the word modify a noun or pronoun? Then choose the adjective. Does it tell how, when, or where? Then choose the adverb.

We are **real/really** proud of our trophy.
Aaron speaks **clear/clearly.**
The Space Shoot is a **safe/safely** ride.
Cross the street **careful/carefully.**
Be **careful/carefully** when you cross the street.
Our basement is **real/really** dark.
This bike rolls **smooth/smoothly** over bumps.
He **sudden/suddenly** came to a screeching halt.

See page 32 for the answers. Don't peek!

A crescent (curve-shaped) moon shines brightly. A half moon shines more brightly, and a full moon shines the most brightly of all. Brightly, more brightly, and the most brightly are all adverbs that modify the verb shines.

CHAPTER TEN

SINGING BADLY, SMELLING GOOD

Congratulations! You're now an expert! You can tell the difference between some very tricky adjectives and adverbs. Now you're ready for the trickiest of them all. They are the adjectives **good** and **bad** and the adverbs **well** and **badly**.

Look at the examples below. The verbs are **speaks, sings,** and **pounces.** Only an adverb can modify a verb. Only an adverb can answer the question "how?" Therefore, only the adverbs—**well** and **badly**—are correct.

EXAMPLE

RIGHT (ADVERB)	WRONG (ADJECTIVE)
Elmer speaks **well.**	Elmer speaks **good.**
Tweety sings **badly.**	Tweety sings **bad.**
Sylvester pounces **well.**	Sylvester pounces **good.**

Get ready to be confused! Things work the opposite way with

linking verbs. Some linking verbs are forms of the verb "to be." They include **am, is, are, was,** and **were.** Other linking verbs are **seem, taste, appear, look, feel, sound,** and **act.**

Use adjectives after linking verbs. Why? Because only adjectives can modify nouns or pronouns. Look at these examples:

EXAMPLE

RIGHT (ADJECTIVE)
Elmer felt **bad** about Bugs.
Tweety looks **bad.**
Sylvester smells **good.**

WRONG (ADVERB)
Elmer felt **badly** about Bugs.
Tweety looks **badly.**
Sylvester smells **well.**

Bad and **good** are adjectives because they modify nouns—Elmer, Tweety, and Sylvester. But **badly** and **well** are adverbs. In the wrong examples above, they modify verbs. Can you see the problem with using adverbs here? You would never say, "Sylvester smells well." That means his nose is working properly!

How to Learn More

At the Library

Cleary, Brian P., and Brian Gable (illustrator). *Dearly, Nearly, Insincerely: What Is an Adverb?* Minneapolis: Carolrhoda, 2003.

Collins, S. Harold, and Kathy Kifer (illustrator). *Adjectives and Adverbs.* Eugene, Ore.: Garlic Press, 1990.

Gregorich, Barbara, and Usborne Books. *Adjectives and Adverbs.* Tulsa, Okla.: EDC Publications, 1999.

Heller, Ruth. *Up, Up, and Away: A Book about Adverbs.* New York: Grosset & Dunlap, 1991.

Terban, Marvin, and Peter Spacek (illustrator). *Checking Your Grammar.* New York: Scholastic, 1994.

On the Web

Visit our home page for lots of links about grammar:
http://www.childsworld.com/links.html
NOTE TO PARENTS, TEACHERS AND LIBRARIANS: We routinely check our Web links to make sure they're safe, active sites—so encourage your readers to check them out!

Through the Mail or by Phone

To find a Grammar Hotline near you, contact:
THE GRAMMAR HOTLINE DIRECTORY
Tidewater Community College Writing Center
1700 College Crescent
Virginia Beach, VA 23453
Telephone: (757) 822-7170
http://www.tcc.edu/students/resources/writcent/GH/hotlino1/htm

To learn more about grammar, visit the Grammar Lady online or call her toll free hotline:
THE GRAMMAR LADY
Telephone: (800) 279-9708
www.grammarlady.com

Fun with Adverbs

Here's a fun exercise. Write sentences with adverbs that

match the action. Examples:

1. Jonathan **tirelessly** changed his tires.

2. April complained about her food **bitingly.**

3. Seth **coolly** opened the freezer.

4. The lamb came along **sheepishly.**

Index

Answers

Answers to Text Exercises

page 18

clearly, more clearly, most clearly

soon, sooner, soonest

happily, more happily, most happily

late, later, latest

cheaply, more cheaply, most cheaply

page 26

really (adverb)

clearly (adverb)

safe (adjective)

carefully (adverb)

careful (adjective)

really (adverb)

smoothly (adverb)

suddenly (adverb)

About the Author

Ann Heinrichs was lucky. Every year from grade three through grade eight, she had a big, fat grammar textbook and a grammar workbook. She feels that this prepared her for life. She is now the author of more than 100 books for children and young adults. She has also enjoyed successful careers as a children's book editor and an advertising copywriter. Ann grew up in Fort Smith, Arkansas, and lives in Chicago, Illinois.